£5 for this love

Stephen Daniels

PaPer
Swans
Press

£5 for this love

First published in Great Britain in 2018
by Paper Swans Press

ISBN 978-1-9998196-7-5

Printed in Great Britain by Jasprint

paperswans.co.uk

Contents

Condition

After I had run you over the third time
my car stopped warning me. The kids
in the street came out and poked you with sticks,
each creating their own stories of how you got there.

You had always been in the middle of our road
which is why I was surprised the day you stood
up and started talking to me.

You used a dialect I didn't fully understand.
I watched your gestures, slipping in and out
of exaggeration and dramatic mime.

After the third attempt at signing your demise
I decided it was best to pick you up and put you back.
I ran over you again to make sure you stayed there
and returned to my empty home.

I can't

wait for me to dry-out
watch as the doctor refuses to pray

scrape this tension from my teeth
not hear that ringing sound

feel sorry when I hit you
forget this faux-nirvana threshold

rely on hallelujah-praising lawyers
cross my trembling fingers

nail myself to your shadow
take your faith-straightened attitude

channel false optimism
hail to the inevitability of falling

understand how many cherry lips I can hold
plant my guilt into them and chew

believe in this broken bread
let it soak in my saliva

accept repentance as the only form of happiness
smash a stained-glass window and put it back together

reasons to run

#1 to escape or hide
i did everything they claimed
all things worth finding are hidden
deeper than most people are willing to search
when i told you my mistakes we both stared lower

#2 liberty or freedom
i am privileged my feet don't hurt
i once ran until my knees started
aching and my leg muscles broke
i felt like you wanted less than i did

#3 pursuit or chase
there was this girl at school
who would squeeze my arm until it hurt
reaching the place you targeted and slowing down
i knew you were close behind which is why i didn't stop

#4 fitness or health
i weighed myself today
i have fat all over my body
but the leanest of limbs
my arms were tired

#5 competition or winning

my best lap time was fifty two seconds

sometimes going around in a circle

is the same as moving forward

a medal is not always a symbol of success

He was a genius

that's how they always described him, able to order
an Indian
takeaway with the smallest of thought,
to answer
the quickest of questions with the sharpest
of movements,
his legs tripped over the air, his arms saved his genius but not
his knees,
I knew him before and he was regular, a packet
of crisps,
he was crunchier than the average bhaji, which is why he avoided
the markets,
he sold his right arm to a cheesemaker, who refused to smell it first,
he started
every sentence with an exclamation mark
and finished
each with a slur, his father was known for his train-like movement, he
left yesterday
two hours early, he started writing this poem in
his sleep,
when he lived – he wanted to grow trees, when he
got young
he wanted to eat greens, sometimes when no one was watching
he stopped.

People with Small Windows

The house peers at me with its squinting
window. Placed just below eye level,
inhabitants stoop to peek through.

I can sense its double-glazed principles
and withstand the reflected glare of the sun
but I struggle to tolerate the fingers
and eyes that point from behind.

Despite its half-hearted efforts to be a real window,
the occupiers fill the space with messages,
facing outwards, to state their position,
and influence other small windowed people.

The shape and size appear fixed
but could they find a bigger window
or is this the window they have chosen?

My house has far-reaching windows,
I often open them to let in the fresh air.
Occasionally I roll down the blinds to a slit
only to find, our plants lean to the right.

Checking In

I check my daily horoscope through internet eyes.
My social status update tells you this.

I check my to do list
you tell me what I must tick next.

I check my social status update
you tell me – *I am not what I say I am.*

I check on the underside of my elbow
your diagnostics are correctly functioning.

Replace your battery.
I check you are still working for me.

My social status posts a political poem,
rages against the previous battery.

I check with real people, my feet start to walk away.

I check my social status, you are not part of my friend group.

I check my photos, you are not in my albums.

I check my identity, you close my eyes.

I try to check everything, you tell me I cannot.

too much Man in this poem

i am a Man
not a Man
but a Man

i am but a Man
a Man not Man

Man
i am a Man
but not a Man

but i am not a Man
i am Man

not a Man
i am Man
but I am

am I a Man
Man but i am not

i am not a Man
but I am

not a Man
i am but i am

i am
i am but i am not

Impatience

He hurried through the supermarket,
searching for time.

A worried glance at fresh fruit left no hints.

The assistant had forgotten where time was kept.
Can anyone who knows
where time can be found, come forward?

nothing.

The Deli counter was not serving slices of time —
people had stopped asking for it.
Now they sold pieces only in joints.

He rushed the meat counter
and there it was, in all its raw savagery.

A slab of time — ready to consume.

At home, he googled
how to prepare time.

One website said to smear it
with sage and cook slow, and long.

Another said sprinkle with pepper,
turn up the heat - bake it quick.

He decided to do neither.

Instead, sat next to his uncooked piece
of time and considered it.

This was the first instance he had spent
any meaningful session with time.

He savoured it, then he ate it all, raw.

He chewed its gristle,
until it passed.

bent metal bench

stretched into shape

each rusted crease
creaks on each seat
solemn strained pose

early years mock
the breaking bars
of burly elders

now its torso waits
for heavy-loaded passengers
to place over-indulged pressure

into every aching scar
to maintain its figure

The Roof Over Our Heads

This lofty position offers no consolation
for a weighted opinion, heavier than a ballot box.

These roofs are built too high
to climb down, ladders out of reach.

One vote used to equal one vote,
now I can see it is worth less.

An exchange rate of diminishing returns,
poverty continues to climb,

real returns are captured
in matured earnings.

The charts trend upwards
when turned upside down,

the long-term figure is positive
through post-truth lenses.

Meanwhile, I am up on the roof
refusing to hum Drifters songs,

sneering at the people below,
who later I will break

as I land – from my ever declining
set of options and eroded principles,

which rush at me faster,
the further I fall.

cheap

this love was battered eventually
it started naked with its scales
shining and its eyes vacant
now they are covered
coated and ready

a flick of batter
to test the temperature
followed by a splash
and disruption of fat
to make this love quickly

the cook wipes his hand
with a stained blue tea-towel
and returns to his till
punching the numbers
with each definite press

£5 for this love

division

during maths class
i wrote on the back of your hand

i want you to stay
a scratched blue mark

that you felt the need to rub away
between english and french the following day

i saw you
indecisive

in the corridor
your hand was red

from where you had spent the morning
removing my love

it was then i realised your intentions
i pleaded with furrowed brow

made clear this was not about our differences
but you simply shrugged off my desires

now we can't share friends
over half are yours

the rest are mine

Everyday Supervillain

I wear an inverted cape
that remains static as I defy the skies.

I use my super strength to twist
bottle tops tighter than most can open.

I spoil ballot papers, to waste the time
of people who have too little.

To counteract virtuous deeds,
I sneer at happiness, in all its guises.

I stare longer than is comfortable,
and tut at overly enthusiastic campaigners.

I refuse to answer questions directly
and often invent words to misdirect meaning.

My supersonic hearing allows me to intrude
on others' conversations – I share other people's secrets.

I sit alone and repeat sound bites.
I spend my days deceiving your trust.

The Inconsiderate Left

My left eye is tearing away, right is going nowhere.
They are not working together these days,
the left is attempting to break free.

A gentle jolt out of the socket,
a thin thread connection to my brain.
Right takes an armchair, stubborn comfortable placement.

A turn here and there is fine but no intent to move.
Right strains to judge depth, without its opposite.

Excess

The man who had three arms

Used the first to lift his heavily medicated problems
The second allowed him to hold his children
The third arm departed while he was sleeping

The man who had three legs

When running, often found himself tripping
Whilst standing, never lost balance with his tripod-like stance
Needed more space than others when sitting crossed-legged

The man who had three ears

Listened carefully to sounds that escaped others mouths
Heard many opinions simultaneously
Rarely said what others thought

The man who had three eyes

Used one eye to pretend to read the news
Moved the second, middle eye, independently to frighten young children
Fixed the third eye firmly on your position

The man who had three cheeks

Turned the first one
Then the second
He thrust his third into your face

The man who had three lungs

Breathed deeper with his first breath
Exposed the volume in his chest with a second
Exhaled for the rest of this life

Rehabilitation — week 6

take my arm and press, open this door and pull the handle,

pull the handle, pull the hand, drag the door, open, move

and keep hold of hand, let loose grip of fingers, thump

your arms and march, bruises ask questions, of the pressure,

fingers resist, sit down, chair takes weight and force up,

push up, resist upwardly mobile, on the floor, horizontal

legs not upright, and scramble, twist arms, through routine

moves and spin, in a corner and brace legs, from laying,

precise legs, scratched in dust, scrape tiles, take tiles

and prise them, snap tiles, arm in hand, resist arm in arm,

resist, on face and leg on tile, and arm in fist, clutch at door

handles and turn away, toes on tiles, lose grip, toes on tiles,

shove, slip, toes on tiles, slip toes, on tiles, slip.

Sleeping with statistics

Next to me rest the 53%
of the morbidly obese male population.
I slide across and begin to stroke their chest,
testing their heartrate -
58 beats per minute, no 85 beats per minute.
2.1 billion in total at last count.

87 out of 100 of their lives will end before mine.

They exhale in unison with their crisp smoker's rasp,
collectively cough,
their lungs offering an even chance
of making it through this lifetime with their own.

There is a 10% likelihood that they will be donors
a further 10% will be operated on by failing doctors.
£52 million a year will save this failing system,
there is a 1% chance of this happening.

They take two minutes out of every hour
(3.33 recurring % of their time)
telling me they will quit tomorrow
but the 63% of the population who recycle, know better.

In the 17 sleep disturbances they experience tonight,
they'll spend around 40 seconds on average
refusing to supply their brains with adequate oxygen.

I stop 67% of the time (2 thirds) to tell them I love them.
I am certain they'll hear it soon.

Changing

We started removing our trousers together
their soaking legs clinging to each limb.

You joked about how trousers only ever come in plural
and a single trouser entered my mind

as you pulled the second leg out
and I saw just your underwear.

Bright as detergent, vivid as my imagination
you stood astride and questioned why I was so slow.

I wanted to take in each moment
and unwrap myself the way I wished it was you.

Your clothes a pile on the floor
you watched me, removing each sock

before you began to re-dress
with each article laid-out in order of size

every one a solitary survivor, separate
and waiting for its complementary garment.

Do you mind if I take these clothes?
You pointed to the meticulously placed set

to my right. *Either is fine* I answered.
Taking in one last look. You began to dress,

pulling the jeans to your waist. Your zip the final act
of this diversion. Your eyes looked down at my top.

Foraging

Golden sultanas

contain as small an amount as half a

sprig and a generous seasoning of

symptoms – including vomiting and diar-

heat. Whisk in the butter and check

in Hanover and in Munster, including

the reducing cooking juices.

The woodlands close to their refugee shel-

pour the rest of the marinade.

40 reported cases, mainly linked

using a heavy kitchen knife, slice

them for the bearded amanita

shred the Kale finely, cook in the

Mediterranean area

gently, then add a little salt and

ing them. It's tragic, particularly when

flesh is still pink and juicy within.

This poem was created using a random method, combining the two articles:

'Refugees fall victim to poisonous mushroom' –
Guardian (Page 19), Wednesday 30 September 2015.

Nigel Slater 'Grilled Partridge, Orange and Lemon Marinade' Recipe –
Observer Food Monthly, September 2015, No. 174 p.24.

Lines were separated according the article and numbered.
Using a numbered spinning wheel and alternating between the two articles.

Some joining words at the beginning and end of the lines were removed
to help with coherence.

Three missed calls and he cried

His voice was on-hold
Please Sir
the *ir*
longer than his plea
stronger than desperation

Dialling tone blink expressions
The *ir* left home
to commute to his deception
I want to talk about your PPI claim

I wanted to swipe his false
c*laim* away to see how he might
sob into his unsheathed handset
and split my 3pm into two

But this time I left too late
Pllleeeeeeeeeaaaaaaaasssee Sirrrrrrrr
He collects cards, direct debits and standing orders
as I exit the conversation

FRIED ONIONS

```
F  I E
F    E D
   I   D
  R  E D
  R I  D
F R        O
F  I  D  O
  R  E D  O
   I  D  O
F          O N
           O N
  R              I O
F                I  N
F R  E          O N
  R  E          I  N
  R  E D  O N I O N
    I       N    N
       D     I  N
           N  O N
     E  O N      S
       D        O N S
```

Moments after separation

Thunder
      clicks
            nearer to prayer

I want the crying to stop

excuse me sir,   she's lost her father
each problem   further   from mine

she wouldn't sleep on the plane
              you should sound the alarm

Is anybody dead?
           I have a problem

look at you,
        I am a
          responsible
              parent

You don't live there anymore
                    it was the right time to leave

close to lightning
          veneer
therapies glazed   in a damaged room

away from confusion
away from faith

Poem

This is a place for truth

This is what a poem looks like

This is a place for mis-trust

This is what a poem sounds like

This is a place to hide

This is what a poem tastes like

This is a place to put your faith

This is what a poem smells like

This is a place to maintain your ego

This is what a poem feels like

This is a place to stutter over political correctness

This is how a poem sees you

This is a place to stop

This is how a poem makes you think

This is a place to undo yesterday

This is how a poem can make you feel

This is a place to unpack thoughts

This is how a poem dresses

This is a place to consider your next move

This is how a poem un-dresses

This is a place to call home

This is why a poem is

This is a place of hope

This is why a poem isn't

This is a place where your worst moments collide

This is why a poem may be

This is a place I can afford

This is why a poem will always be

This is a place for others

This is a poem

This is a place

Routine Excuses

'The happiness of most people is not ruined by great catastrophes or fatal errors, but by the repetition of slowly destructive little things' - Ernest Dimnet

But I didn't break today.

I wanted to break around 11am.
But I needed to finish that report.

I thought I might break at 2pm.
But then I had a meeting.

It seemed I would break at 5pm.
But the kids needed food.

I was ready to break at 10pm.
But politics, austerity, gender discrimination, racism, obesity, nationalism, buttons, egos, the legal system, Lords – oh lordy lords, the 52%, PIPs, the casual decline of social standards, refugees, big hands, experts, small hands, democracy, drowning, poems – so many poems, stereotypes, capitalism, identity, gender identity, national identity, my identity, and did I leave the back door unlocked.

Tomorrow I will find the time to break.

Feed the poets

The more I write,
the less I seem to say.

My sex is understood
by those who don't have sex.

My gender is underappreciated.

I've had this cold for over 16 years
there aren't enough tissues to last me a day.

My nose is Roman.
my identity is unclear.
All I know is what the radio tells me.

My shipping forecast is brighter
than the front of my house
which smells of lavender
and tastes of dog day afternoons.

Please help me write more poems.

Just one line of poetry
could nourish me for over a year.

A whole stanza
has been known to raise eyebrows.

Giving a complete poem will result in changed attitudes
throughout the poetry community.

Population 3,862 and declining.

I used to think if I ate an apple core, a tree would grow in my belly

Day 1

A pip nestles in my stomach,
finds a fertile space to settle.

Day 2

Sprouts appear,
show signs of growth.
I send down much needed water.

Day 5

It craves sunbeams
and other apple saplings –
at what point does it become a tree?
They say an apple tree can take 20 years to grow full size.

Day 274

I have these lines
and blemishes on my face.
Lemon trees can develop needing
only a little light. An apple tree cannot mature without
sunlight. My body obliges. As I fall asleep, I feel the bark forming.

Day 4,222

I can feel the branches
rustling around my lungs.
I coughed yesterday: a leaf appeared.
The roots irritate my knees; I woke this morning
and moved too quickly leaving a crick in my neck –
I could hear my twigs snapping. Appetite slows as more apples fruit.

Day 7,300

My skin feels thicker,
more rough. Teenagers often visit,
spend their afternoons kissing under
my cover, carve their initials into my torso
before they depart. My head feels hazy, I struggle
to peer through the blossom in my eyes. I will keep them
closed today. They say apple trees can live for over 100 years - 36,500 days.

Fathered

I am not my Father's eyebrows
of Swallows nest

I am not my Father's simmering testosterone
his slapping self-belief

I am not my Father's mental arithmetic
his cash balance or his overdraft

I am not my Father's drinking
his 2-litre Sunday afternoon measure
his pint of emotional instability

I am not my Father's weight gain
I try not to be his self-control
his control or his self

I am not my Father's sense of humour
I could never be as sharp-eyed
or wit-tipped

I am not my Father's boarding school
I am not his failed parents
their precise cutlery

I am not my Father's weight loss
his scan of approval
his tumour-ridden discipline-tests

I am not my Father's abuse
I did not allow myself to understand
his rope-burned neck

I am not my Father's factory job
I am not his 16-hour days
I will never be his child avoiding child

I am not my Father's unshaven face
his razor-sharp judgment
his sensitive pride

I am not my Father's pocket comb
I am not the constant checking
I am not his receding hairline

I am not my Father's cooking skills
his bacon scraped pans and lard lined evenings
I am not his insistence to deep fry his mistakes

I am not my Father's food bank
his wait in line
his racist slur

I am not my Father's

If that were a practice in poetry

after Louisa Campbell

I would buy it
and frame it,
if that were a practice in poetry

I would douse it
in sugar and eat it

I would dip it
in chocolate sauce
and share it

I would take it
to the highest building
throw it off
watch it
drift over minds

I would risk it
all on the river

I would place it
on the head
of the kindest person
exclaim what a wonderful hat.

I would tie it
to the leg of a carrier pigeon
set it free.

I would lose it
in a maze –
so others could find it

I would race it
in a marathon
a marathon number of times

I would leave it
on the cheek of my loved ones
ask them to cherish it.

I would challenge it
to a duel
let it win

I would write it
on a page and publish it.

I would put it
in a book and love it

I would love it
if that were a practice
in poetry

Acknowledgements

Acknowledgements are due to the editors of the following publications in which some of the poems, or versions of, have appeared: The Interpreter's House, Eye Flash Poetry, Ink Sweat and Tears, Atrium Poetry, Riggwelter, I am not a silent poet, Picaroon Poetry, Perverse Poetry, The Open Mouse, Nutshells and Nuggets, Domestic Cherry, The Curly Mind and The Fat Damsel.

***

Stephen Daniels is the editor of Amaryllis Poetry (www.amaryllispoetry.co.uk). His debut pamphlet, *Tell Mistakes I Love Them* was released by V. Press in 2017.

His poetry has been widely published in numerous magazines and websites, including The Interpreter's House, Obsessed With Pipework, Ink Sweat & Tears, Perverse Poetry, Elbow Room, And Other Poems, The Lake, Clear Poetry, Atrium Poetry, Picaroon Poetry, The Fat Damsel, Three Drops from a Cauldron, Eunoia Review, Algebra of Owls, The Open Mouse, I am not a silent poet, Good Dadhood, The Poetry Shed, Spilling Cocoa Over Martin Amis, The Curly Mind and Nutshells and Nuggets.

His poems have also appeared in several anthologies including Richard Jefferies Writers – '78 Anthology, Domestic Cherry, Ink Sweat & Tears *12 Days of Christmas* 2016 and his poem 'Light' was runner-up in the Candlestick Press micropoem competition 2015.

www.stephenkirkdaniels.com

@stephendaniels